# AL-FURQAN
## Clear Signs For Those Who Reflect

Compiled by:
Muzammil Siddiqi

Edited by
Al-Bayyinah

 AI-BAYYINAH

Al-Bayyinah
PO Box 6613
Nottingham NG2 7YN
United Kingdom

Published in the UK by Al-Bayyinah

First Published in May 2006


Typeset in Palatino 10/14 [CP]

*A copy of the British Library Cataloguing in Publication data is available from the British Library*

ISBN 0-9553011-0-6
ISBN 978-0-9553011-0-0

Printed and bound in Turkey by Mega Printing

# CONTENTS

|  | Introduction | viii |
|---|---|---|
|  | Biography | ix |
|  | Glossary | x |
| 1. | Surah Al-Fatihah | 13 |
| 2. | Surah Al-Baqarah | 13 |
| 3. | Surah 'Al 'Imran | 18 |
| 4. | Surah Al-Nisa | 20 |
| 5. | Surah Al-Ma'idah | 22 |
| 6. | Surah Al-An'am | 23 |
| 7. | Surah Al-A'raf | 25 |
| 8. | Surah Al-Anfal | 27 |
| 9. | Surah Al-Tawbah | 28 |
| 10. | Surah Yunus | 29 |
| 11. | Surah Hud | 30 |
| 12. | Surah Yusuf | 31 |
| 13. | Surah Al-Ra'd | 32 |
| 14. | Surah Ibrahim | 33 |
| 15. | Surah Al-Hijr | 33 |
| 16. | Surah Al-Nahl | 34 |
| 17. | Surah Al-Isra' | 35 |
| 18. | Surah Al-Kahf | 36 |
| 19. | Surah Maryam | 37 |
| 20. | Surah TaHa | 38 |
| 21. | Surah Al-Anbiya' | 39 |
| 22. | Surah Al-Hajj | 40 |
| 23. | Surah Al-Mu'minun | 41 |
| 24. | Surah Al-Nur | 41 |
| 25. | Surah Al-Furqan | 42 |
| 26. | Surah Al-Shu'ra' | 43 |
| 27. | Surah Al-Naml | 44 |

| 28. | Surah Al-Qasas | 44 |
| 29. | Surah Al-'Ankabut | 45 |
| 30. | Surah Al-Rum | 46 |
| 31. | Surah Luqman | 47 |
| 32. | Surah Al-Sajdah | 47 |
| 33. | Surah Al-Ahzab | 48 |
| 34. | Surah Saba' | 49 |
| 35. | Surah Fatir | 49 |
| 36. | Surah Yasin | 50 |
| 37. | Surah Al-Saffat | 50 |
| 38. | Surah Saad | 51 |
| 39. | Surah Al-Zumar | 52 |
| 40. | Surah Ghafir | 53 |
| 41. | Surah Fusilat | 54 |
| 42. | Surah Al-Shura | 54 |
| 43. | Surah Al-Zukhruf | 55 |
| 44. | Surah Al-Dukhan | 56 |
| 45. | Surah Al-Jathiyah | 56 |
| 46. | Surah Al-Ahqaf | 57 |
| 47. | Surah Muhammad | 57 |
| 48. | Surah Al-Fath | 58 |
| 49. | Surah Al-Hujurat | 58 |
| 50. | Surah Qaf | 59 |
| 51. | Surah Al-Dhariyat | 59 |
| 52. | Surah Al-Tur | 60 |
| 53. | Surah Al-Najm | 60 |
| 54. | Surah Al-Qamar | 61 |
| 55. | Surah Al-Rahman | 61 |
| 56. | Surah Al-Waqi'ah | 62 |
| 57. | Surah Al-Hadid | 63 |
| 58. | Surah Al-Mujadalah | 64 |
| 59. | Surah Al-Hashr | 64 |
| 60. | Surah Al-Mumtahinah | 65 |

| 61. | Surah Al-Saff | 65 |
| 62. | Surah Al-Jumu'ah | 66 |
| 63. | Surah Al-Munafiqun | 66 |
| 64. | Surah Al-Taghabun | 67 |
| 65. | Surah Al-Talaq | 67 |
| 66. | Surah Al-Tahrim | 68 |
| 67. | Surah Al-Mulk | 68 |
| 68. | Surah Al-Qalam | 69 |
| 69. | Surah Al-Haqqah | 69 |
| 70. | Surah Al-Ma'arij | 69 |
| 71. | Surah Nuh | 69 |
| 72. | Surah Al-Jinn | 70 |
| 73. | Surah Al-Muzammil | 70 |
| 74. | Surah Al-Mudathir | 70 |
| 75. | Surah Al-Qiyamah | 70 |
| 76. | Surah Al-Dahr | 70 |
| 77. | Surah Al-Mursalat | 70 |
| 78. | Surah Al-Naba' | 71 |
| 79. | Surah Al-Nazi'at | 71 |
| 80. | Surah 'Abasa | 71 |
| 81. | Surah Al-Takwir | 71 |
| 82. | Surah Al-Infitar | 72 |
| 83. | Surah Al-Mutaffifin | 72 |
| 84. | Surah Al-Inshiqaq | 72 |
| 85. | Surah Al-Buruj | 72 |
| 86. | Surah Al-Tariq | 72 |
| 87. | Surah Al-A'la | 73 |
| 88. | Surah Al-Ghashiyah | 73 |
| 89. | Surah Al-Fajr | 73 |
| 90. | Surah Al-Balad | 73 |
| 91. | Surah Al-Shams | 74 |
| 92. | Surah Al-Layl | 74 |
| 93. | Surah Al-Dhuha | 74 |

94.    Surah Al-Inshirah                      74
95.    Surah Al Tin                           74
96.    Surah Al-'Alaq                         74
97.    Surah Al-Qadr                          75
98.    Surah Al-Bayyinah                      75
99.    Surah Al-Zilzal                        75
100.   Surah Al-'Adiyat                       75
101.   Surah Al-Qari'ah                       75
102.   Surah Al-Takathur                      75
103.   Surah Al-'Asr                          76
104.   Surah Al-Humazah                       76
105.   Surah Al-Fil                           76
106.   Surah Quraish                          76
107.   Surah Al-Ma'un                         76
108.   Surah Al-Kawthar                       76
109.   Surah Al-Kafirun                       77
110.   Surah Al-Nasr                          77
111.   Surah Al-Lahab                         77
112.   Surah Al-Ikhlas                        77
113.   Surah Al-Falaq                         77
114.   Surah Al-Nas                           77

INTRODUCTION

All praise is to Allah, and may peace and blessings be upon our Prophet Muhammad, and upon all his family and companions. "It is He who sent to an illiterate people a messenger from amongst them, reciting to them His signs and purifying them and teaching them the Book and wisdom even though before they were in clear error" (62:2).

The Qur'an is the revelation of Allah's own words for the guidance of Mankind. Since the Qur'an is the primary source of Islamic teachings, the correct understanding of the Qur'an is necessary for every Muslim.

This book 'Al-Furqan' gives a brief summary of all the chapters in the Qur'an, and outlines the key points in a concise format, enabling the reader to quickly appreciate the contents of the Qur'an, chapter by chapter, and for those more familiar with the Qur'an it acts as an aide-mémoire.


PUBLISHER'S NOTE

Al-Bayyinah was founded to provide Islamic products to the Muslim community, primarily focused on Qur'an studies. The proceeds are used to fund charity work.

We are delighted to present to new Muslims and all English-speaking Muslims the book 'Al-Furqan', a brief summary of the Qur'an. May Allah guide us all to the Straight Path, the Path of those upon whom He has bestowed His Grace, not those upon whom His Wrath falls, nor those who are astray —Aameen.

## Brief biography of Dr Muzammil Siddiqi

Dr. Siddiqi received his BA in Islamic & Arabic Studies from the Islamic University of Madinah, Saudi Arabia in 1965. He later went on to complete a degree in Comparative Religion at Harvard University in 1978. Currently, Dr. Siddiqi works as an Educator and Religious Director of the Islamic Society of Orange County, where he has served since 1981.

Presently, Dr. Siddiqi is serving as a member of the ISNA Majlis Ash-Shura and the Fiqh Council of North America. He has also served as chairman of the Religious Affairs Committee and has been a member of the Board of Trustees of the National American Islamic Trust (NAIT) for the past six years. As a member of the Executive Board of Majlis al-Shura of Southern California, Dr. Siddiqi has organized and participated in several national and international Islamic conferences on Sirah, Fiqh and Da'wah. Because of his devotion to the preservation of Islam in America, he has organized numerous training programs for Muslim adults and youth. He also lectures on Islam and interfaith dialogue in North America and abroad.

Dr. Siddiqi has authored books on Hajj & Umra and Ramadan.

He has published many academic papers and articles in encyclopaedias and journals as well as his weekly column in Pakistan Link. Since 1982, he has provided Qur'an commentary in a weekly radio program.

Dr. Siddiqi served as the president of ISNA from 1996—2000.

Dr. Siddiqi, originally from India, now resides in Fountain Valley California.

| Arabic (transliteration) | English equivalent |
|---|---|
| Allah | God |
| Musa | Moses |
| Haroon | Aaron |
| Du'a | Supplication |
| Iblis | Satan |
| Tawrat | Torah |
| Injil | Scriptures sent down to Jesus |
| 'Ad | People of Hud |
| Thamud | People of Salih |
| Halal | permitted |
| Haram | prohibited |
| Isra' | Prophet Muhammad's night journey from Makkah to Jerusalem |
| Mi'raj | Prophet Muhammad's ascension to the heavens |
| Hijrah | Migration (to Medina) |
| Mushrikun | Polytheists |
| Tawhid | Monotheism |
| Ummah | Nation |
| Shirk | Polytheism |
| Saba' | Sheba |
| Risalah | Message |
| Akhirah | Hereafter |
| Dawud | David |
| Sulaiman | Solomon |
| I'lyas | Elias |
| Yunus | Jonah |
| Ibrahim | Abraham |
| Ishaq | Isaac |
| Yaqoub | Jacob |
| Ismail | Ishmael |
| Al-Yasa' | Elisha |

| | |
|---|---|
| Zulkifl | A prophet of the Arabs whose story is like that of Ezekiel |
| Da'wah | Invitation to Islam |
| Nuh | Noah |
| Jinn | Unseen creatures of fire, some Muslim others satans |
| Iman | Belief |
| Taqwa | piety |
| 'Iddah | Time period a widow must observe after her husband passes away |
| Zakaria | Zachariah |
| Salih | Prophet to people of Thamud |
| Hud | Prophet to people of 'Ad |

## 1. SURAH AL-FATIHAH
*Commentary on Surah Al-Fatihah*

This is the first Surah of the Qur'an, although not the first in the order of revelation. It was revealed to the Prophet—peace be upon him—in Makkah in the early period of his mission. This Surah has seven verses.

The Surah is both a Du'a (supplication) and an introduction to the Qur'an. It teaches the basic principles of Islamic faith. All praise and thanks are to Allah, the Lord of all the worlds. Allah is most merciful and most compassionate. Allah is also the Master of the Day of Judgment. We should pray to Allah only and seek His help. We seek His guidance and help to walk on the straight path. This is the path of those who received Allah's favours, not the path of those who incurred His anger or went astray.

## 2. SURAH AL-BAQARAH

Surah Al-Baqarah: This is the longest Surah of the Qur'an. It has 286 verses divided into 40 sections. This Surah was revealed in Madinah. The Surah deals with a number of issues related to beliefs, history, law and morality. The Surah begins with the statement that it is Allah who revealed this book (the Qur'an) for the guidance of those who are conscious of Allah. Only those who seek guidance can benefit from the guidance of the Quran. Humans are three types:

• First are those who believe in the unseen realities, perform prayers, give part of their wealth in charity, and believe in what is revealed in this scripture and what was revealed before to other prophets and messengers of Allah. These are the true believers. They shall benefit from the Quran and shall be eternally successful.

• Second are those who decided to reject Allah's message—the disbelievers. Since they have made up their minds to reject Islam, no preaching will help them. Allah will punish them on the Day of Judgment because of their rejection.

• Third are those people who say that they have believed, but actually have not. They try to be on both sides: sometimes on the side of faith and sometimes on the side of disbelief. They are the hypocrites. They may think that in this way, they will win over both sides, but in reality they are the losers.

All people are invited to worship Allah and become His true servants. Allah created all people and He made the earth and heaven for their benefit and produced sustenance for them. The problem comes when people deny their Creator, break the relations that Allah told them to keep, follow the wrong ways in life and make mischief in the land.

The story of the creation of human beings is told. Allah created Adam. He gave him knowledge, asked angels to bow to him and gave him and his wife the garden of bliss to reside in, and enjoy its fruits. He told them to eat whatever they wished, but not approach one tree. However, Satan caused Adam to lose paradise. Allah sent Adam and his wife to earth and told them to remember the lesson that they had learnt in Paradise: They need Allah's guidance. Satan is their worst enemy. Those who obey Allah on this earth will return to Paradise, but those who obey Satan may end up in hell.

Allah's covenant with the children of Israel is mentioned. It is mentioned that those who receive Allah's covenant must live by it.

Allah blessed those who fulfil their promise to Him. Prophet Ibrahim's (Abraham) prayer, the Ka'bah's importance and the coming of Prophet Muhammad is also mentioned. The command to change the direction of prayer from Jerusalem to the Ka'bah emphasized the final covenant of Allah with Prophet Muhammad and his followers. The Surah also speaks about basic beliefs, acts of worship, economic dealings, morals and manners. The rules of marriage, divorce and 'iddah are mentioned. The Surah discusses many subjects.

### Commentary on Surah Al-Baqarah

1. The Quran is the Book of Guidance for those who want to be righteous. The difference between the believers and non-believers.

2. The hypocrites: their sickness, mischief and self-deception.

3. Mankind, worship Allah alone and make no partners in Allah's divinity. The challenge of the Qur'an. This Book will guide many but many will remain in error. The character of those who shall remain in error.

4. The story of the creation of Adam. Allah's plan and promise to send His guidance from time to time through His prophets.

5. Address to Bani Israel to accept this message. Allah's covenant must be fulfilled.

6. Warnings to those who stray from the covenant of Allah. How some from among the Children of Israel turned away from Allah's teachings.

7. Allah's blessings on the Children of Israel and their transgressions.

8. The real recipients of Divine salvation. The hesitation of Bani Israel in sacrificing the cow.

9. Some perversions of those who were supposed to follow the law of Allah.

10. Basic principles of Allah's Covenant with the Children of Israel.

11. How some of them were too arrogant to follow the teachings of their prophets, some rejected the prophets or tried to kill them, some worshipped the calf, disobeyed Allah's commands and became too greedy for the life of this world.

12. Opposition and enmity towards the Prophets, following devils and magic.

13. Reminders to the Believers not to follow these examples. Stay firm on your principles. Some among the People of the Book will try to mislead you with false claims and assertions.

14. The true guidance of Allah is here. Read the Book of Allah and follow it.

15. The great example of Prophet Ibrahim (Abraham)—peace be upon him. He and his son built the Ka'bah and prayed for a Prophet to come.

16. Prophet Ibrahim (Abraham)—peace be upon him—submitted to Allah and this is the message that he and his sons gave to their progeny.

17. The change of Qiblah and the response of the hypocrites and fools. Those who have knowledge know that this is the true Qiblah of all the Prophets.

18. Follow this direction wherever you are. This is the universal Qiblah for all.

19. Believers will be tried but they should be firm and steadfast and must face trials with patience and prayers.

20. Allah's signs and His bounties are everywhere. The polytheists and idolaters misplace their loyalties.

21. Believers should eat good and permissible food and should never follow the steps of the devil.

This part of Surah al-Baqarah begins with Ayat al-Birr. It talks about true piety. True piety is not turning the face to the east or west. It is not just some rituals and doctrines. It is total commitment to Allah. After this rules related to fasting, Hajj, war and peace, marriage and divorce are mentioned. The real purpose of these laws and rules is to cultivate piety in the life of individuals and justice in society.

22. True piety and righteousness. Some rules related to the punishment of murderers. The rules of bequests.

23. Fasting and Ramadan: the objective of fasting and some rules.

24. Rules of Hajj, fighting those who expelled Muslims from their homes.

25. No fighting during Hajj, rather seek Allah's bounty when you return from Hajj.

26. Appreciate Allah's bounties. All human beings were originally one community. Divisions came later. Be generous and defend yourself and your faith.

27. Some important questions answered: War in the sacred months, wine and gambling, charity, orphans' money, divorced women and their situation.

28. The laws of divorce.

29. Continuation of the laws of divorce.

30. Rules on the remarriage of the divorced women or the widowers.

31. Further rules of divorce.

32. Fighting in the cause of Allah: two examples from history; the Israelites under the leadership of Prophet Musa (Moses).

33. Under the leadership of Prophet David—peace be upon him—the victory over the forces of Goliath.

34. Emphasis on charity. To Allah belongs everything. His Throne extends over heaven and earth. No compulsion in religion. Allah brings people out from darkness into light.

35. Allah's power over life and death, some examples: Prophet Ibrahim's (Abraham) dialogue with Namrood, a man in the valley of dead (probably Prophet Ezekiel's vision of Jerusalem), Prophet Ibrahim (Abraham) asks Allah how He will raise the dead to life. Allah's answer to Prophet Ibrahim (Abraham).

36. Allah blesses charity: examples of how Allah blesses charity.

37. Emphasis on charity: spend good things; give openly and secretly to the poor and needy.

38. Prohibition of usury (Riba); its bad effects on persons and society.

39. Some rules on loan transactions.

40. Conclusion and prayer: Everything in the heaven and earth belongs to Allah, the prayer of the believers.

### 3. SURAH 'AL 'IMRAN

This is the 3rd Surah in the Qur'an according to its arrangement, but it is 89th Surah according to the order of revelation. It is a Madani Surah. This means that it was revealed after the Hijrah, some part of it was revealed in the 3rd year of Hijrah and some later.

'Al 'Imran means "the family of 'Imran". Imran was the father of Prophets Musa (Moses) and Haroon (Aaron)—peace be upon them. There are references in this Surah to these two great Prophets of Allah and then the story of Mary and birth of Jesus is mentioned. The main topics of this Surah are Tawhid, Prophethood and the truth of the Qur'an. As Surah al-Baqarah discussed the issues related to Bani Israel, this Surah discusses issues related to the Christian community and its religious positions. It also discusses Hajj, Jihad, Zakat and Riba. It ends, like Surah al-Baqarah, with a Du'a (supplication). This Surah consists of 200 verses divided into 20 sections.

### Commentary on Surah 'Al 'Imran

1. Allah is the Ever-Living, Self-Subsisting. He sent the Qur'an as He sent before the Tawrat (Torah) and Injil (the scripture sent down to Jesus) for the guidance of people. True believers are those who accept everything from the Book of Allah and try to understand it. Believers always pray for Allah's guidance to them.

2. Those who reject the truth, then their wealth and their progeny will not avail them against the chastisement of Allah.

3. Allah bears witness that there is none to be worshipped but Him (Tawhid), as well as the angels and the people of knowledge. The religion acceptable in the sight of Allah is Islam.

4. To love Allah one must follow the Prophet. Obedience to Allah and His Messenger are necessary for faith. Allah chose Adam, Noah, Family of Ibrahim (Abraham) and the Family of Imran to guide humanity through them. Many prophets and messengers of Allah came for this purpose.

5. The birth of Jesus—peace be upon him—and his true message.

6. Jesus preached the message of Tawhid. His true followers are those who accept Tawhid. Jesus' birth was miraculous, just as Adam's was miraculous. Some Christians argued with the Prophet. He invited them to an open Mubahalah (i.e. solemn meeting).

7. Invitation to the People of the Book to come to a common word of Tawhid and obedience to Allah.

8. Some People of the Book try to discredit Islam. Muslims are warned to be conscious of this challenge.

9. Previous prophets and their scriptures confirm the truth of Islam.

10. Charity and sacrifice are necessary to attain faith and piety. Muslims should pay attention to the Ka'bah and stand firm to give the message of Islam to the world.

11. Muslims must remain conscious of Allah and must hold fast together the rope of Allah, i.e. His Book and His guidance.

12. Role of the Muslim Ummah in the world.

13. Critical review of the Battle of Uhud.

14. Prohibition of Riba and emphasis on charity. Believers must hasten to seek the forgiveness from their Lord. Some beautiful characters and qualities of the believers are mentioned.

15. Prophet Muhammad is only a Messenger of Allah like other messengers. His death should not mean giving up the faith. Believers must persevere and be patient in difficulties.

16. Criticism of those who showed weakness during the Battle of Uhud. Muslims should be strong in their commitment to faith.

17. True believers and the hypocrites. The hypocrites' delinquency at the time of Uhud.

18. Steadfast attitude of the Believers. Satan tries to frighten the Believers, but true Believers are strengthened by trials and tests.

19. Some propaganda of the People of the Book against Islam and how to respond to such challenges.

20. Allah's promise of success for the Believers. How the believers should pray to Allah and seek His blessings.

### 4. SURAH AL-NISA

This is a Madani Surah revealed to the Prophet—peace be upon him—between the years 3 and 5 of Hijrah.

There are three main themes in this Surah:

• Establishment of the new Islamic social order after removing the pre-Islamic system.

• Answers to the oppositions of Pagan Arabs as well as neighbouring Jews and Christians.

• Da'wah of Islam to new people.

This Surah consists of 176 ayat divided into 24 sections.

### Commentary on Surah Al-Nisa

1. Responsibility to take care of the family. Special care of orphans.

2. Laws of inheritance. It is an obligation from Allah.

3. Relations between men and women should be based on the principle of equity and goodness.

4. Rules of marriage especially concerning the women who cannot be taken in marriage.

5. Men and women's rights over their properties.

6. Disagreement and reconciliation between husband and wife.

7. Internal and external purity: rules of wudu, ghusl and prayers.

8. Fulfil the trusts and refer all disputes to Allah and His Messenger.

9. Those who decline to accept the decisions of Allah's Messenger are the hypocrites.

10. It is the duty of the Believers to establish justice and protect the poor and oppressed.

11. The hypocrites' attitude to the Prophet and to the Believers.

12. How to deal with the hypocrites who are prone to fighting.

13. Believers must respect the life of other Believers. Murder and its punishment.

14. Believers must join and live with other Believers unless they are unable to do so.

15. Prayers for the travellers and those who are in the battlefield.

16. Always be just and do not take the side of the unjust.

17. The secret councils of the hypocrites.

18. Allah will not forgive Shirk. Satan's misleading of humans through deceptions and false promises.

19. Some more directions about dealing with orphans and family disputes.

20. Believers must stand for justice for all. They must pay attention to their faith.

21. Hypocrites try to deceive Allah. They are lazy in their prayers. Their end will be the lowest part of hell.

22. Allah's punishment for those who broke their covenant with Him. Some People of the Book tried to crucify Jesus; Allah saved him.

23. The message of Islam is the same as that of previous Prophets.

24. Invitation to the People of the Book to accept Islam and recognize the true teachings of Jesus. Elaboration on the law of Inheritance.

## 5. SURAH AL-MA'IDAH

This is the 5th Surah according to the arrangement of the Qur'an and 112th according to the order of revelation. It was revealed in Madina soon after the Treaty of Hudaibiyah either towards the end of the 6th year of Hijrah or at the beginning of the 7th year of Hijrah. In this Surah there is a verse (5:3) that is believed to be the last verse revealed to the Prophet—peace be upon him. The Surah consists of 120 verses in 16 sections.

There are six main points discussed in this Surah:

•All obligations whether they are divine or human should be ful-filled. When we have a pledge or promise or sign a treaty we must abide by it. Also Allah gave some rules for life to keep us clean and sober. Cleanliness of the body, living with justice, being upright and moral, avoiding sin, corruption and superstition, and doing the deeds of piety and righteousness are important rules and principles and must be observed.

• Message to the People of the Book i.e. Christians and Jews to rec-ognize the truth. Allah's punishment comes on those who reject Allah's rules and knowingly violate them.

• The story of the two children of Adam is told. This story has many lessons. Sometimes even your brothers become envious and harm you. Just and righteous persons sometimes suffer at the hands of their own family members, but Allah's judgment comes. The right-eous must always show correct attitude and behaviour.

• Muslims must deal with justice with all people. Justice should be impartial; even to their enemies they must be just. However, rela-tions among Muslims themselves should be deeper. There should not only be justice, but also love, brotherhood, care and concern for each other.

• Enjoy the good things that Allah has given, but guard against excesses. Do not indulge in swearing, gambling, intoxicants, super-stition, and violation of the sanctities of the Sanctuary of Allah (the Ka'bah).

- Jesus—peace be upon him—was a great prophet of Allah. He performed many miracles, but his teachings were not followed and were corrupted after his departure from this earth.

## Commentary on Surah Al-Ma'idah

1. General Rules of Discipline.

2. Cleanliness for prayers, Command to abide by justice.

3. Allah's covenant with the Children of Israel.

4. Children of Israel broke the covenant of Allah.

5. Musa (Moses)—peace be upon him—warned the Children of Israel.

6. Story of the two children of Adam, Punishment for the offenders.

7. Allah's rules must be established.

8. The relations of Muslims with their opponents.

9. Those who make mockery of the truth.

10. How Christians deviated from the truth.

11. Some Christians came closer to Islam and recognized the truth.

12. Prohibition against intoxicants, gambling and shirk.

13. Respect of the Ka'bah.

14. Rules against idolatry and about testimony.

15. Some miracles of Jesus—peace be upon him.

16. How the teachings of Jesus were corrupted after his departure.

## 6. SURAH AL-AN'AM

This is the 6th Surah according to the arrangement of the Qur'an and 55th Surah according to the order of revelation. This Surah was revealed in Makkah about one or two years before the Hijrah. The Surah has 165 verses in 20 sections.

In this Surah, the message of Tawhid is highly emphasized. It contains basic principles of Tawhid. It gives beautiful description of Allah's creative power. It criticizes Shirk and its manifestations. Basic topics discussed here are:

• Unity of Allah is the reality in this universe.

• Polytheism has no foundation.

• Prophet Ibrahim (Abraham)—peace be upon him—preached Tawhid. Other Prophets also gave the same message.

• Allah's judgment will come and the truth will prevail.

• Allah gives right guidance about food and other matters of life.

### Commentary on Surah Al-An'am

1. Allah created the heaven and earth, but the non-believers make others equal to Allah.

2. The punishment of Allah came upon those who denied the truth.

3. On the Day of Judgment, the Mushrikun (i.e. those who joined gods with Allah) will admit their guilt.

4. Those who deny the Hereafter are the real losers. Non-believers ridiculed Allah's Prophets, but in the end the truth prevailed.

5. Nations were warned before. Allah did try them in various ways.

6. Believers should be respected.

7. Allah is the Final judge and He will decide the destiny of the individuals or nations.

8. The power and might of Allah.

9. Prophet Ibrahim's (Abraham) arguments against Shirk.

10. Other Prophets also gave the message of Tawhid.

11. Allah's revelation to His Prophets.

12. Allah's signs in the creation.

13. Allah has no partner, no son.

14. Arrogance of the non-believers and their opposition to the Prophets. Do not eat the animals slaughtered in the name of other than Allah.

15. Those who plot against Allah, they suffer themselves.

16. Superstitions of the Mushrikun (i.e. those who joined gods with Allah).

17. Allah's gifts for humanity and people's self-imposed prohibitions.

18. What are the things that Allah has forbidden?

19. Universal principles of Islam.

20. The true religion: prayer, sacrifice, life, death, everything must be for Allah.


## 7. SURAH AL-A'RAF

This is the 7th Surah of the Qur'an and according to some authorities it is the 39th Surah according to the order of revelation. This Surah was revealed in Makkah about a year or two before the Hijrah. It consists of 206 verses in 24 sections.

The basic theme of this Surah is Risalah, i.e. Allah's message as it was sent through many messengers. Several Prophets and parts of their stories are mentioned to emphasize Prophets' mission and their struggle with their people. The Surah tells us that Allah's Prophets suffered for the cause of truth. Their enemies tried to harm them, but then Allah helped his prophets and defeated their enemies. The Surah emphasizes that the true message must be presented under all circumstances. After the Prophets, it is the duty of the Believers to convey the message of Allah to all people.

### Commentary on Surah Al-A'raf:

1. The Qur'an is revealed to remind the believers and to warn humankind about the consequences of their actions. The judgment will indeed take place.

2. The story of Man's creation and Satan's opposition to Man.

3. Warning to the Children of Adam to be aware of Satan's plots.

4. Allah's messengers came to guide people.

5. End of those who denied and those who accepted the message.

6. Cries of the wicked in the hellfire.

7. The righteous shall prosper.

8. Lessons from the story of Prophet Noah—peace be upon him.

9. Some lessons from the story of Prophet Hud—peace be upon him.

10. Some lessons from the story of Prophets Salih and Lot—peace be upon them.

11. Lessons from the story of Prophet Shu'aib—peace be upon him.

12. Warnings against those who deny the Prophets and Messengers of Allah.

13. Prophet Musa (Moses)—peace be upon him—and his encounter with Pharaoh of Egypt.

14. Pharaoh and his magicians were defeated.

15. Pharaoh continued in his persecution of the Israelites.

16. Some more signs were shown to Pharaoh and his people.

17. The Tawrat (Torah) was given to Prophet Musa (Moses)- peace be upon him.

18. Some Israelites started calf worship.

19. The Tawrat (Torah) and Injil (the scripture sent down to Jesus) speak about the coming of Prophet Muhammad—peace be upon him. Allah's promise for those who will follow the last Prophet.

20. Prophet Muhammad is the Universal Prophet. Some among the people of Prophet Musa (Moses) were guided by the truth and lived with justice.

21. Some Israelites transgressed Allah's laws and they suffered the consequences.

22. The eternal covenant of Allah taken from all human beings.

23. The coming of the Last Hour.

24. Shirk has no logic. Ignore the wrongdoers, but invite to Allah with kindness. Listen to the Qur'an and always remember Allah.

## 8. SURAH AL-ANFAL

The 88th Surah according to the order of revelation. This is a Madani Surah revealed soon after the Battle of Badr in the 2nd year of Hijrah (or 624 CE). This Surah has 75 verses in 10 sections.

The Surah reminds the Believers to obey Allah and His Messenger and keep good relations with each other. It gives rules of war and peace between Muslims and their enemies. In this Surah, Allah has addressed Muslims six times with "O you who believe" (see vs. 15; 20; 24; 28; 29; 46).

### Commentary on Surah Al-Anfal

1. Commandment relating to the spoils of war. Battle of Badr.

2. Allah's help for the Believers in the Battle of Badr.

3. Believers must always obey Allah and His Messenger.

4. Only the righteous should be the guardians of the Masjid al-Haram (the Ka'bah) in Makkah.

5. The purpose of war and the rules about the distribution of the spoils of war.

6. Be firm and united in combat against the enemy.

7. Victory of the Believers against the unbelievers. Allah does not change His blessings unless people change themselves.

8. Always be prepared to defend yourself and your people. Make peace if the enemy is inclined towards peace.

9. Allah's promise to help the Believers.

10. Treatment of the prisoners of war and obligations towards Muslims living among non-Muslims.

### 9. SURAH AL-TAWBAH

Surah 113 according to the order of revelation. This is a Madani Surah revealed in the 9th year of Hijrah after the Battle of Tabuk. It has 129 verses in 16 sections.

The basic subjects of the Surah are: The non-believers who broke their treaties, Muslims have no obligation to honour treaties with them. Muslims must protect themselves from hypocrisy, weak faith and negligence. Battle of Tabuk and its lessons.

### Commentary on Surah Al-Tawbah

1. Proclamation that the Treaty of Hudaibiyah is cancelled.

2. Honour the treaties with those who honour them. Fight with those who have broken the treaty.

3. Mushrikun (i.e. those who joined gods with Allah) are forbidden to be the caretakers of the Masjid al-Haram.

4. Muslims should trust Allah, not just their numbers.

5. Jews and Christians also committed Shirk. Command to spend in the path of Allah. The correct number of months.

6. The Tabuk expedition.

7. Those who stayed behind and did not participate in the Battle of Tabuk, hypocrites and weak in faith.

8. The proper distribution of charity. Those who speak ill of the Prophet or make fun of Allah and His Book.

9. The hypocrite men and women.

10. Jihad against the unbelievers and hypocrites who attacked Islam and Muslims.

11. Severing of all ties with the hypocrites.

12. Genuine Muslims who needed exemptions from the battle. The hypocrites who made lame excuses.

13. The hypocrites and their plots against the Believers.

14. The true Believers and their characteristics.

15. Be always with those who are truthful.

16. Prophet Muhammad is a kind and compassionate person and he is deeply concerned for the well-being of the Believers.

### 10. SURAH YUNUS

Surah 51 according to the order of revelation. This Surah was revealed in Makkah perhaps a few years before the Hijrah. It has 109 verses in 11 sections.

The main subject of this Surah is faith in Allah and belief in the Hereafter. Those who have true faith, worship Allah and recognize Him as their Lord and Master and live their lives in accordance to His command. Allah sent His Messengers to remind people and to warn them. The stories of Prophets Noah and Prophet Musa (Moses) with Pharaoh are told to remind people about the consequences of disbelief and arrogance.

### Commentary on Surah Yunus

1. The Qur'an is the Book of wisdom with signs from the All-Wise.

2. Man's ingratitude to Allah and His revelation.

3. Allah's mercy to His creation. Allah invites to the abode of peace.

4. Allah's gifts. The Qur'an is from Allah. Bring a Surah like the Qur'an if you can.

5. Those who disbelieve in the Qur'an shall be the losers. Every people were sent a Messenger.

6. The Qur'an is a mercy, blessing and cure for mankind's problems.

7. Whatever you do Allah is a Witness. The mistakes of the Mushrikun (i.e. those who joined gods with Allah) .

8. The story of Prophet Noah and his people. Prophet Musa (Moses) and Haroon (Aaron)—peace be upon them all.

9. Allah delivered the Children of Israel from bondage of Pharaoh.

10. Allah's mercy for the Children of Israel. Prophet Yunus and his people.

11. If Allah afflicts you with any loss or wants to bestow any profit on you, none can avert it. You must always follow Allah's guidance.

## 11. SURAH HUD

Surah 52 according to the order of revelation. This is a Makki Surah revealed soon after the previous one. It has 123 verses in 10 sections. In this Surah, we have the stories of Prophets Noah, Salih, Hud, Lot, Shu'aib and Musa (Moses)—peace be upon them all. The basic point is that Allah sent His Prophets and Messengers to mankind out of His grace and mercy, but when people did not listen to the Prophets and rejected their message, Allah's punishment was relentless. It makes no difference whether someone was the son of a Prophet, his wife or anyone, none shall escape Allah's judgment.

### Commentary on Surah Hud

1. Seek forgiveness from Allah and His bounties will be for you.

2. Patience and good deeds bring the stability in character.

3. The story of Prophet Noah—peace be upon him.

4. The fate of those who disbelieved in Prophet Noah. The moving description of the fate of Prophet Noah's son.

5. The Message of Prophet Hud. 'Ad people denied Allah's message and were punished.

6. The Message of Prophet Salih; the She-Camel and end of Thamud.

7. Prophet Ibrahim (Abraham) receives the angels. The angels then went to Prophet Lot. The punishment of the people of Lot—peace be upon him.

8. Prophet Shu'aib and his message, his people's denial and their punishment.

9. Prophet Musa (Moses) was sent to Pharaoh and his people. The purpose of these stories.

10. Prophets were denied before. Continue presenting the message with patience. Had Allah forced His will upon the people, He would have made them all one people.

## 12. SURAH YUSUF

It is a Makki Surah revealed towards the end of the Makkan period, about a year or two before the Hijrah. This Surah has 111 ayat in 12 sections.

The basic theme of the Surah is to emphasize that all Prophets were human beings and their messages were similar. They were also highly moral beings. This is the way all believers should be. The Prophets trusted in Allah and in the end, Allah's plans gave success.

### Commentary on Surah Yusuf

1. Prophet Yusuf's dream.

2. Prophet Yusuf suffered the bad treatment of his stepbrothers.

3. Prophet Yusuf was sold in Egypt, his firm piety faced temptations.

4. Prophet Yusuf in prison.

5. Prophet Yusuf preaches to the inmates.

6. The King's dream and Prophet Yusuf's interpretation.

7. Prophet Yusuf was cleared of the false charges against his character. He became a high official in Egypt.

8. Famine in Palestine brought Prophet Yusuf's brothers to Egypt.

9. Prophet Yusuf meets his real brother.

10. Prophet Yusuf disclosed his identity to his stepbrothers.

11. Prophet Jacob's family comes to Egypt. Prophet Yusuf honours his parents and forgives his brothers.

12. In the histories of the Prophets, there are many lessons for us to learn and follow.

### 13. SURAH AL-RA'D

The 96th Surah in the order of revelation. Opinions differ about its being a Makki or Madani Surah. According to some authorities it is Makki with the exception of few verses and according to others it is Madani except few verses revealed in Makkah. It seems its time period is closer to the Hijrah. The Surah has 43 verses in 6 sections. The basic theme of the Surah is divine guidance. Allah has created this whole universe. He knows what is in the wombs and everything comes under His knowledge. He sent His prophets and guides to all people for their guidance and now the Last Messenger has come.

*Commentary on Surah Al-Ra'd*

1. Allah's signs in nature.

2. Allah knows everything; the whole universe praises Him. Those who have eyes can see the truth. The truth has an abiding power.

3. The faithful and disbelievers, their characters and their ends.

4. The comfort of the hearts is in the remembrance of Allah. Those who deny Allah, no signs or miracles can help them.

5. People in the past also denied Allah's Prophets and laughed at them, but what were their ends.

6. Prophet Muhammad is the Messenger of Allah. The witness is Allah and all those who have knowledge of the Scriptures of Allah.

## 14. SURAH IBRAHIM

The 72nd Surah in the order of revelation. It is probably one of the last Makki Surahs. It has 52 verses in 7 sections.

The basic theme of the Surah is Allah's guidance through His prophets. The purpose of this guidance is to take the people from darkness to light. Many people in the past had doubts about their prophets. They laughed at them and they threatened to kill them or expel them from their towns. However, the lasting word is the "good word." The Surah also mentions Prophet Ibrahim's (Abraham) prayer when he established the city of Makkah.

### *Commentary on Surah Ibrahim*

1. The purpose of the Qur'an is to lead humankind to light.

2. Prophets and their people.

3. Non-believers threatened the Prophets, but Allah's promise to the Prophets was fulfilled.

4. Satan misleads the disbelievers in this world, but in the hereafter, he leaves them in the lurch.

5. The ingratitude of people.

6. Prophet Ibrahim's (Abraham) prayer for Makkah, for its people and for his own children.

7. Allah is aware of the acts of wrongdoers; their respite and end.


### 15. SURAH AL-HIJR

The 54th Surah in the order of revelation. This is a Makki Surah revealed about 3-4 years before the Hijrah. It has 99 verses in 6 sections. The name al-Hijr refers probably to the same area where Thamud used to live in the north-western part of Arabia.

The Surah's main theme is divine guidance, and people's response. Allah's warns those who deny this message and reminds of these warnings in the stories of Prophet Lot's people, Thamud and others.

*Commentary on Surah Al-Hijr*

1. The Qur'an is the Book of Allah. He revealed it and shall guard it.

2. Allah knows everything in the universe. He is the Creator of all.

3. The creation of the human being is from very humble stuff, but Allah honoured him and asked angels to bow down to Adam. Satan's response.

4. Allah is very forgiving, but His punishment is also severe.

5. Prophet Lot and Prophet Shu'aib's people.

6. The People of Hijr and what happened to them. Qur'an and Surah al-Fatihah are special gifts of Allah. Allah will take care of those who ridicule His message.

**16. SURAH AL-NAHL**

The 70th Surah in the order of revelation. This is one of the late Makki Surahs revealed sometime before the Hijrah. This and the previous six Surahs (Yunus, Hud, Yusuf, al-Ra'd, Ibrahim and al-Hijr) were revealed one after another. The time period and themes are similar. This Surah has 128 verses in 16 sections. The Surah speaks about Allah's creative power. Everything in the universe points to Allah. There is coherence and balance in Allah's creation.

*Commentary on Surah Al-Nahl*

1. The whole creation points to Allah.

2. The truth is that there is only One God.

3. The reward of the righteous and the disgrace of the wicked.

4. Allah's message has come. Man is a creature of Allah, but he argues a lot.

5. The Mushrikin's argument and the answer.

6. Prophets were human beings. The mission of the last Prophet. Warnings to non-believers.

7. Prohibition against Shirk. Arabs used to call angels the daughters of Allah, yet they themselves did not like to have daughters.

8. Allah gives time to people to repent and turn to him.

9. Consider the bounties of Allah. Some more signs mentioned.

10. The comparison between the faithful and the disbelievers.

11. Warnings about the Last Hour. Allah's favours to humankind.

12. Prophet Muhammad is a witness over all witnesses.

13. Justice, benevolence, care of kith and kin are Allah's commands. He forbids shameful deeds, evil and aggression.

14. The Qur'an was sent by Allah, even the Prophet cannot make any changes to it.

15. Every soul will be paid in full what it has earned. Halal (permitted) and Haram (prohibited) are the authority of Allah.

16. The ideal faith of Prophet Ibrahim (Abraham). The best way of giving Da'wah.

**17. Surah Al-Isra'**
Surah 50 in the order of revelation. This is a Makki Surah revealed after the events of Isra' and Mi'raj, which took place about a year and half before the Hijrah. The Surah has 111 verses and 12 sections. This Surah concentrates on some important moral and spiritual principles. It emphasizes that human beings always need divine guidance. Without the guidance of Allah, humans end up in evil, sin and misery. Human beings must have good relations with each other and live in a society built on the principles of faith, justice and morality. The Surah talks about the evils of pride and arrogance and urges human beings to reflect on Allah's signs and be humble before Him in prayers.

## Commentary on Surah Al-Isra'

1. Isra' journey of the Prophet to Jerusalem and the history of that area.

2. Human beings are hasty. Reward and punishment all have their time.

3. Moral and spiritual principles are emphasized—Worship of Allah and respect of parents.

4. Moral principles—children's rights, decency, right of life, orphans' property, honesty in dealings, humbleness.

5. Tawhid is the basic message of the Qur'an.

6. Gentleness is enjoined.

7. Satan's pride pitted against man, and his pledge to mislead man.

8. Every one will be brought on the Day of Judgement with his/her own deeds.

9. Emphasis on prayers, and on reading the Qur'an.

10. The Qur'an is inimitable.

11. Non-believers have lame arguments for rejecting the Prophets.

12. The attitude of Pharaoh towards Prophet Musa (Moses) and the signs that he showed.

### 18. Surah Al-Kahf

The 69th Surah in the order of revelation. This is a Makki Surah revealed 4-5 years before the Hijrah. It has 110 verses in 12 sections. The Surah answers some questions that the Mushrikun of Makkah posed to the Prophet—peace be upon him. The answers came in a very clear way and also challenged them to accept the message of Islam. In this Surah, we have the stories of: the People of the Cave, the man who had two gardens and was very proud of himself, Prophet Musa (Moses) with an angelic figure, Dhul-Qarnain a pious ruler. These stories are told to emphasize the value of faith, knowledge and patience, the relativity of time, and the variety in this world.

## Commentary on Surah Al-Kahf

1. The straight message of the Qur'an.

2. The Companions of the Cave.

3. The proof of resurrection.

4. Always remember of Allah. Everything depends on Allah's will.

5. The parable of an ungrateful person and a grateful person.

6. Wealth and children are only a passing show.

7. Satan and his progeny are the declared enemies of human beings.

8. Allah's mercy is available all the time.

9. Prophet Musa's (Moses) search for a teacher.

10. Some strange events and their explanations.

11. The pious ruler Dhul-Qarnain. Gog and Magog.

12. The real losers and winners.

**19. SURAH MARYAM**
This Surah was revealed in Makkah sometime before the first Hijrah to Abyssinia, which was about 8 years before the Hijrah to Madina. The Surah has 98 verses in 6 sections.
The subject matter of this Surah is the true message and teachings of the Prophets of Allah. Several Prophets are mentioned: Zakariyya, Yahya, Isa and his mother Maryam, Ibrahim (Abraham), Musa (Moses), Ismail and Idris—peace and blessings of Allah be upon them all. Allah blessed these Prophets. They taught Tawhid and called their people to the worship of Allah alone. Great miracles and signs were also shown in the lives of these Prophets and Messengers.

*Commentary on Surah Maryam*

1. Prophet Zachariah's prayer for a son. Birth of John (Yahya) and Allah's favours upon him.

2. Maryam—peace be upon her—and the miraculous birth of her son Jesus—peace be upon him.

3. Prophet Ibrahim (Abraham) preached the unity of Allah. His conversation with his father.

4. Other great Prophets and Messengers of Allah.

5. The Resurrection will surely happen.

6. Criticism of misconceptions on intercession and divinity of Jesus.


## 20. SURAH TAHA

This is a Makki Surah. It was revealed sometime before the Hijrah to Abyssinia. It is also mentioned that the recitation of this Surah by 'Umar's sister led to his conversion to Islam. This took place sometime in the 5th year of Prophethood. This Surah has 135 verses in 8 sections.

The subject matter of the Surah is to assure the Prophet and his followers that the message of the Qur'an will eventually succeed. The story of Prophet Musa (Moses) is mentioned in detail. It then mentions how the enemies of Islam oppose it and what the consequences of this opposition will be for them.

*Commentary on Surah TaHa*

1. Prophet Muhammad is told not to feel distress because of the denial of the disbelievers. Allah knows everything. Remember the story of Musa (Moses). Allah called him to the Prophethood and gave him special signs.

2. Prophet Musa's (Moses) prayer. Allah commanded Musa (Moses) and his brother Haroon (Aaron) to go to Pharaoh and give him the message. Allah mentions His favours upon Musa (Moses).

3. Prophet Musa (Moses) goes to Pharaoh. Challenge of the Egyptian magicians. Defeat of the magicians and then their conversion.

4. Allah saved the Children of Israel from Pharaoh. Prophet Musa (Moses) goes to Sinai. Samiri misleads the Israelites and they worship the calf.

5. The anger of Prophet Musa (Moses). Samiri confessed his evil action and was punished.

6. The Day of Judgment. No intercession will help without Allah's permission. The opponents of the Prophet.

7. Satan misleads human beings. The story of Adam and Iblis (Satan).

8. Evil doers will be punished. Be patient and offer regular prayers.

**21. SURAH AL-ANBIYA'**
The 73rd in the order of revelation. This is a Makki Surah revealed about 5-6 years before the Hijrah. It has 112 verses in 7 sections. The basic theme of the Surah is Prophets and Prophethood as indicated by the name itself. All Prophets were human beings. They suffered at the hands of their enemies. Allah tested them, but they always trusted Allah and lived according to His command. They were people of prayers and devotions; Allah listened to their prayers.

*Commentary on Surah Al-Anbiya'*
1. The Last Messenger has come. The judgment is coming closer. All prophets were human beings.

2. Heaven and earth are created for a purpose. All Prophets preached Tawhid.

3. Everything is created for a term. The end will come suddenly.

4. Allah cares for you, Muhammad, day and night. Musa (Moses) and Haroon (Aaron) received Allah's message and now this blessed reminder has come to Muhammad.

5. Prophet Ibrahim (Abraham) argued against idolatry.

6. Allah blessed His Prophets and delivered them.

7. The righteous shall inherit the earth.

## 22. SURAH AL-HAJJ

The 103rd according to the order of revelation. Some authorities consider this a Makki Surah, but according to the majority it is Madani. This Surah has 78 verses in 10 sections.

The Surah reminds about the approaching end of the world, need for the firmness of faith to support the truth and to eradicate the evil. It talks about prayers, humbleness, sacrifice, respect of the Ka'bah—the House of Allah, and striving to defend the truth.

### *Commentary on Surah Al-Hajj*

1. The Quake of the Last Hour. Arguments for the Resurrection from the stages of human creation and from the rain that produces vegetation.

2. The marginal believers and their end.

3. The true believers shall be rewarded.

4. Pilgrimage to the House of Allah.

5. Respect for the Symbols of Allah.

6. Permission for fighting back is granted to those to whom wrong is done. The real purpose of Jihad.

7. Satan's enticements and Allah's especial protection of His words.

8. The reward of those who migrate in the cause of Allah.

9. Allah's order prevails in the heaven and earth.

10. The Muslim community is chosen by Allah for a special purpose.

## 23. SURAH AL-MU'MINUN

This is an early Makki Surah revealed about 6 7 years before the Hijrah. It has 118 verses in 6 sections.

In this Surah, people are invited to accept and follow the Prophet. This is the central theme of the Surah. It speaks about the character of true believers and assures that they will be the truly successful people. It draws attention to various stages of human creation, to many other universal signs. Then it takes stories of other prophets and tells us that they also preached the same message.

### Commentary on Surah Al-Mu'minun

1. The character of the Believers. Various stages of human creation and Allah's signs in the universe.

2. The Message of Prophet Noah, his people's response and the flood.

3. Generations were raised after Prophet Noah. Many prophets were sent among them. Then came Prophet Musa (Moses) and Haroon (Aaron) and then came Jesus—peace be upon them all.

4. All prophets are one Ummah and preached the same religion. Those who are affluent think that they are also the righteous people, but the righteous are only those who do good deeds.

5. Everything in the heaven and earth belongs to Allah.

6. The Prophet's job is to continue presenting the message of Allah. This life is the only chance. This life has a purpose.

## 24. SURAH AL-NUR

This is a Madani Surah revealed around the 6th year of Hijrah after the Battle of Mustaliq. It has 64 verses in 9 sections.

This Surah contains many rules for development of a society based on righteousness and morality. It talks about male-female relations, rules of proper dress for Muslim women, rules for punishment of adultery and those who accuse others of adultery or fornication.

## Commentary on Surah Al-Nur

1. Punishment of adultery. Rules of testimony in case of adultery.

2. The false rumours against 'Aisha—may Allah be pleased with her.

3. Beware of those who slander pious chaste women.

4. Rules about entering others' homes, and proper dress. Help those who are single get married.

5. The light of Allah and the struggle between light and darkness.

6. Everything in the heaven and earth glorifies Allah.

7. Believers must obey Allah and His messenger. Allah's promise to the Believers to establish them in the land.

8. Rules of privacy for men and women, at home and outside.

9. Especial respect of the Prophet and Believers' duties towards him.

### 25. SURAH AL-FURQAN

This is a Makki Surah revealed around the middle Makkan period about 6-7 years before the Hijrah. It has 77 verses in 6 sections. The Surah answers some of the objections of the non-believers against the Qur'an and the teachings of Islam. It also presents the character of the Believers as criteria to prove the truth of Islam.

## Commentary on Surah Al-Furqan

1. Prophet Muhammad is a Warner for the whole world. Evil of Shirk. Objections of those who denied the Prophet and his message.

2. The Punishment of those who deny Allah and His message.

3. Non-believers' demand to see the angels or Allah. Non-believers question why the whole Qur'an was not sent down at once.

4. Examples of the people of Prophets Musa (Moses), Haroon (Aaron), Noah and 'Ad, Thamud and the People of al-Rass (a town probably in Yamamah).

5. Examples from the natural world: shadows, night and day, rain-bearing winds, oceans with two types of waters, creation of human beings, creation of the heaven and earth in six days.

6. The character and qualities of the most faithful servants of Allah.

### 26. Surah Al-Shu'ra'

This is a Makki Surah revealed in the middle Makkan period about 6-7 years before the Hijrah. It has 227 verses in 11 sections.

The non-believers asked for signs to prove the Qur'an was the word of Allah. Allah mentioned many signs both in nature and in history. The stories of many prophets show they all had the same message.

### Commentary on Surah Al-Shu'ra'

1. Allah has power to bring down the mightiest sign, but here is a test for people. This wonderful creation is a sign in itself for those who want to learn.

2. Signs were shown to Pharaoh.

3. Pharaoh's magicians and Prophet Musa (Moses).

4. The exodus of the Israelites from Egypt. The sea parting and giving them passage.

5. Prophet Ibrahim's (Abraham) struggle against idolatry.

6. Prophet Noah and his people.

7. The people of 'Ad and Prophet Hud -peace be upon him.

8. The people of Thamud and Prophet Salih -peace be upon him.

9. Prophet Lot -peace be upon him—and his people.

10. Prophet Shu'aib -peace be upon him—and his people.

11. The Qur'an is the message from the Lord of the worlds. It is not from devils nor have they any clue. It is not poetry of poets, but serious message with eternal consequences.

**27. SURAH AL-NAML**

This is a Makki Surah, probably revealed soon after the previous Surah. It has 93 verses in 7 sections.

The theme of the Surah is divine guidance in history. Allah sent His Prophets to different people. Some accepted them and were guided, while others denied them and they saw the consequences of their denial. The Surah also contrasts between the principles of Tawhid, and Shirk.

### Commentary on Surah Al-Naml

1. The Qur'an is from the All Wise and All-knowing. How Prophet Musa (Moses) received the message of Allah. Allah gave Musa (Moses) many signs, but Pharaoh and his people denied them.

2. The knowledge and power that Allah bestowed on Prophets David and Solomon. What kind of character they had.

3. Queen of Saba' (Sheba) and her submission to Prophet Solomon.

4. The response of Thamud to Prophet Salih's message. Also the example of the people among whom Prophet Lot was sent.

5. The contrast between the Tawhid and Shirk. Allah or the so-called gods of Shirk.

6. The surety of Resurrection.

7. The coming of the Day of Judgment.

**28. SURAH AL-QASAS**

This is a Makki Surah most likely revealed after the previous Surah in the middle Makkan period. It consists of 88 verses in 9 sections. The basic theme of this Surah is prophethood. Some aspects of the life of Prophet Musa (Moses)—peace be upon him—are mentioned to show the similarity between him and Prophet Muhammad —peace be upon all the prophets of Allah. There are also answers here to the questions and doubts raised by some non-believers.

## Commentary on Surah Al-Qasas

1. The story of Musa (Moses) and Pharaoh is related Pharaoh was persecuting the Israelites. Allah wished to show his favour to the oppressed people. Birth of Musa (Moses) and then his growing up in Pharaoh's own palace.

2. Musa's encounter with an Egyptian and his escape to Madyan.

3. Musa's (Moses) marriage in Madyan.

4. Musa (Moses) receives Prophethood and especial signs from Allah. His appearance before Pharaoh. Pharaoh's denial and then Allah's punishment of him and his armies.

5. The Prophet relating these stories by inspiration from Allah and for a purpose.

6. Allah's guidance is continuous.

7. The message of Islam is Tawhid.

8. The story of Qarun: his character and his end.

9. Allah's promise to the Believers.


### 29. SURAH AL-'ANKABUT

This is a Makki Surah, probably revealed in the early Makkan period before the migration to Abyssinia. It has 69 verses in 7 sections. This Surah reminds the Believers to be strong in their faith and not give it up because of hardship, or family pressures. Stories of previous Prophets and their followers are mentioned here to show that the path of truth is not an easy one, but has trials and hardships.

## Commentary on Surah Al-'Ankabut

1. Tests and trials are part of faith.

2. Examples of Prophets Noah and Ibrahim —peace be upon them.

3. Example of Prophet Lot—peace be upon him.

4. Example of Prophet Shu'aib. References to the people of 'Ad, Thamud, Qarun and Pharaoh. Message of Prophet Musa (Moses)—peace be upon him. Spider web of Shirk.

5. Give the message of Allah in the best way.

6. Warnings to the non-believers.

7. The truth will succeed. Allah guides the steps of those who follow the right path.

### 30. SURAH AL-RUM

This is a Makki Surah and it was revealed about 5 years after the Prophethood, in the same year in which the first Hijrah to Abyssinia took place. The Surah has 60 verses in 6 sections.

The Surah reminds us that Allah is in control of everything. Those who are short-sighted see only what is apparent; they do not realize that there is a Creator and Master of this whole universe and it is He who is governing everything. The final decision is in Allah's hand. The Akhirah (hereafter) will take place and the truth will prevail.

*Commentary on Surah Al-Rum*

1. The defeat of the Romans (by the Persians), but their victory later on is foretold.

2. Creation and Resurrection belong to Allah. Glorify Allah at different times of the day.

3. The signs of Allah in nature.

4. The true religion corresponds and enhances the nature. Teachings of the religion of nature: Tawhid, care of the family and relatives, economic justice and charity.

5. Corruption caused by human beings. Evidence of corruption in history. Evidence of resurrection in nature.

6. The Day of Resurrection.

## 31. SURAH LUQMAN

This is an early Makki Surah, revealed perhaps before Surah al-'Ankabut. It has 34 verses in 4 sections.

In this Surah, Tawhid is emphasized, and Shirk and its ideas are critically examined. It tells us that those following Shirk are only blindly following their forefathers. The true wisdom is to believe in Allah. The advice of Luqman—the wise, is also given here to support the same principles.

### Commentary on Surah Luqman

1. Qur'an is a book of guidance and mercy for all people.

2. The advice of Luqman, the wise man.

3. Signs of Tawhid in the heaven and earth. Shirk or polytheism has no basis.

4. In crisis, people turn to the Real God. Let not the things of this world deceive you. All knowledge belongs to Allah.

## 32. SURAH AL-SAJDAH

This is a Makki Surah revealed in the middle Makkan period. It has 30 verses in 3 sections.

The Surah discusses some of the doubts and arguments of the non-believers against the principles of Tawhid, Risalah and Akhirah (hereafter). It invites human beings to think and reflect on their own selves and on nature surrounding them. Everything points to a Wise and Powerful Creator of this universe. He has not created all these phenomena in vain. The creation has a purpose.

### Commentary on Surah Al-Sajdah

1. The Qur'an is from the Lord of the Worlds. Allah created this whole universe. He created human beings, but some human beings deny the resurrection.

2. The difference between the Believers and non-Believers.

3. The Mission of Prophet Musa (Moses)—peace be upon him. Take lessons from the history of other nations. Signs of resurrection in nature.

### 33. SURAH AL-AHZAB

This is a Madani Surah revealed sometime in the 5th year of Hijrah. It has 73 verses in 9 sections.

The Surah deals with a number of social and political issues. It talks about the practice of child-adoption, some marriage customs, the battle of Ahzab and Bani Quraidah, social issues related to Hijab of Muslim women. It also talks about the hypocrites and their conduct in society.

### *Commentary on Surah Al-Ahzab*

1. The custom of adoption and Islamic instructions about it. Prophet Muhammad—peace be upon him—is dearer to the believers than their own selves.

2. The Battle of Ahzab and the way of the hypocrites.

3. Prophet Muhammad, the excellent role model.

4. The household of the Prophet, his pious wives.

5. Allah's rewards for the Believing men and women. The Prophet's marriage to Zainab. The finality of the Prophethood.

6. Prophet Muhammad—peace be upon him—is sent as a witness, a bearer of glad tidings and Shining Lamp. The marriages of the Prophet: certain privileges and restrictions.

7. Rules of conduct in domestic relations.

8. Rules of Hijab, Warnings to the hypocrites, the Last Hour.

9. Believers must speak the truth. Man assumes the burden of trust.

## 34. SURAH SABA'

This is a Makki Surah revealed to the Prophet—peace be upon him—sometime in the early or middle Makkan period about 7-8 years before the Hijrah. It has 54 verses in 6 sections.

The Surah answers some of the objections raised by non-believers about Tawhid, Risalah and Akhirah (hereafter). It also speaks about Prophets David and Solomon, and the Queen of Sheba to remind people about the consequences of evil, as well as righteousness.

### Commentary on Surah Saba'

1. The Day of Judgment will surely come.

2. Allah's favours on Prophets David and Solomon. Allah's judgement on the people of Saba'.

3. Shirk (associating partners with Allah) will be of no use on the Day of Judgment. Prophet Muhammad is sent for all people.

4. The wrong leaders will abandon their followers on the Day of Judgment, their mutual recrimination discussed.

5. Material riches do not necessarily bring you closer to Allah.

6. The truth will prosper.

## 35. SURAH FATIR

This is a Makki Surah revealed sometime in the middle period of the Prophet's residence in Makkah. This Surah has 45 verses in 5 sections.

In this Surah, Allah warns the non-believers of their negative attitude towards Islam and Prophet Muhammad—peace be upon him. The basic message is also explained to them.

### Commentary on Surah Fatir

1. Allah's creative power and His angels. None can stop the mercy of Allah. Beware of Satan.

2. The success of the truth over falsehood will surely come.

3. Allah has power to remove you and bring another group in your place. Every people had a Warner.

4. The true believers in Allah.

5. Allah's plan cannot be altered. Allah gives people time to repent.

### 36. SURAH YASIN

This is a Makki Surah revealed sometime in the middle Makkan period. It has 83 verses in 5 sections.

The Surah explains some of the basic beliefs of Islam, especially the belief in life after death and the Akhirah (hereafter).

### *Commentary on Surah Yasin*

1. The truth of the Qur'an and the truth of Prophet Muhammad—peace be upon him.

2. Allah's messengers were sent to other people. The response of those to whom the prophets were sent and the result of their denial.

3. Allah's signs in nature to remind about the day of Resurrection.

4. The scenes of the day of Resurrection.

5. Reminders about death and the Day of Judgment.

### 37. SURAH AL-SAFFAT

This is a Makki Surah and it was revealed sometime in the middle Makkan period. It has 182 verses in 5 sections.

The Surah speaks about the unity of Allah in very strong terms. It talks about the teachings of various prophets of Allah; all preached the same message. It warns the disbelievers that their plots against the message of Islam will not work. The truth shall prevail.

## Commentary on Surah Al-Saffat

1. The Lord of the heaven and earth is one God. Those mocking the Prophet of Allah will one day see the truth. The Day of Judgment shall dawn suddenly.

2. The guilty shall be punished, and the virtuous rewarded.

3. Allah delivered Prophet Noah from his enemies. Prophet Ibrahim's (Abraham) encounter with idolatry. The test of Prophet Ibrahim. His willingness to sacrifice his son.

4. How Allah delivered Prophets Musa (Moses), Haroon (Aaron), Elias and Lot and punished their enemies.

5. How Prophet Yunus was delivered from the belly of the whale. Angels are not Allah's daughters, but Allah's servants. Allah's messengers shall succeed.

## 38. SURAH SAAD

This is a Makki Surah of 88 verses in 5 sections, revealed around the time of the first Hijrah to Abyssinia about year 5 of Prophethood. The Surah talks about the basic message of all the Prophets and Messengers of Allah. They came to preach Tawhid. The Prophet suffered great hardship in presenting Allah's message. Their enemies attacked and persecuted them, but finally the truth prevailed, and falsehood was defeated. Power and riches all come from Allah. With power some people become arrogant. Allah gave the examples of David and Solomon who were great prophets as well as powerful kings. They obeyed Allah. Their riches did not corrupt them.

## Commentary on Surah Saad

1. Warnings to the disbelievers. The arguments of the disbelievers against the Qur'an and the Prophet. The defeat of the disbelievers.

2. Remember Allah's servant Prophet David. Allah's blessings upon him. He was tested and he turned to Allah.

3. Allah's blessings upon Prophet Solomon. He was also tested, but he repented and was forgiven by Allah.

4. Allah tested Prophet Job and he was rewarded for his patience. Remember Allah's servants: Abraham, Isaac, Jacob, Ishmael, Elisha and Zulkifl. The warnings for the wicked.

5. There is only one God. The great message. Allah created Adam, but Iblis (Satan) became his enemy. He vowed to mislead humans. Allah's curse came upon him and upon those who follow him.

### 39. SURAH AL-ZUMAR

This is a Makki Surah. It was revealed most probably sometime before the Hijrah of Abyssinia. It has 75 verses in 8 sections.

The Surah talks about the true religion; it is to serve Allah sincerely and avoid Shirk. Tawhid brings the blessings of Allah, while Shirk has terrible consequences. The Believers are told not to despair and lose heart. If it is difficult for them to practice their religion in a place, they can migrate from it. The unbelievers are told that whatever they do, shall not turn the Believers away from the path of faith.

### Commentary on Surah Al-Zumar

1. To Allah belongs the pure and sincere religion. The principle of Tawhid and its benefits. The evil of Shirk and its consequences.

2. The reward of those who are steadfast in their faith.

3. The perfect guidance of the Qur'an—straight with no crookedness.

4. Allah is sufficient for the Prophet. The rejecters will be abased.

5. The futility of Shirk and its evil consequences.

6. Allah's mercy is available for all.

7. You ignorant people, do you invite me to worship someone other than Allah? The Judgment of Allah.

8. The reward of Believers and the punishment of the unbelievers.

## 40. SURAH GHAFIR (also known as AL-MU'MIN)

This is a Makki Surah—one of seven (Ghafir, Fusilat, al-Shura, al-Zukhruf, al-Dukhan, al-Jathiyah, al-Ahqaf) beginning with the word "HaMim", and are called "al-Hawamim". All these are Makki Surahs and they were revealed one after another after the previous Surah al-Zumar, in the middle Makkan period before the Hijrah to Abyssinia. This Surah has 85 verses in 9 sections.

These are Surahs of Da'wah, inviting people to believe in Allah, and take advantage of the mercy of Allah. There is solace and comfort in these Surahs for the Believers who were persecuted because of their faith, and are given the good news that the truth will prevail.

### Commentary on Surah Ghafir

1. The Qur'an is from Allah who is both Merciful and Severe in Punishment. Warnings to the non-believers and comfort to the believers.

2. The failure of the disbelievers. The Day of Judgment is Allah's.

3. A lesson from the history of Prophet Musa (Moses)—peace be upon him. Even the mighty Pharaoh and his army could not withstand the wrath of Allah.

4. A believer from the Pharaoh's people declared his faith. His conversation with his people.

5. The false leaders will take their people to hell.

6. Allah helps the Prophets and their followers.

7. The Glory of Allah. Allah has power over life and death.

8. The fate of the un-believers will be bad.

9. Take lessons from the past history. After the judgment comes, repentance makes no difference.

**41. SURAH FUSILAT (also known as HAMIM AL-SAJDAH)**
This is a Makki Surah. See the introduction to the previous Surah.
This Surah has 54 verses in 6 sections.
The subject matter of this Surah is Da'wah. It invites to the truth,
gives warnings to those who reject the truth, and tells us that the
appeal to the truth is within our nature. It tells us also that the
Believers receive strength from Allah's revelation. The revelation
gives life to those who were spiritually and morally dead at one time.
The Surah contains both good news and warnings.

*Commentary on Surah Fusilat*
1. Invitation to the truth of the Qur'an; The Qur'an is a book that
   explains everything.

2. Allah created the heaven and earth. Warnings to those who turn
   away from Allah.

3. Those who deny Allah, their own body will testify against them.

4. The disbelievers who plan to suppress the message of the Qur'an
   will fail. Allah gives strength to the Believers.

5. The best people are those who invite to Allah. The effect of the
   revelation on the Believers. The signs of Allah.

6. Allah gives time to people to repent. What good or evil you do is
   for and against your own selves. The truth will gradually succeed.

**42. SURAH AL-SHURA**
This is a Makki Surah and it belongs to the group of seven HaMim
Surahs that were revealed one after another in the middle Makkan
period. This Surah has 53 verses in 5 sections.
The Surah emphasizes that the message of the Qur'an is from Allah
Who revealed similar messages to other Prophets and Messengers.
The religion of Allah has been the same throughout history. If Allah
wanted He would have made all people one Ummah, but He has

given freedom to people to make their own choice of their free will. Allah will judge all people on the Day of Judgment. In the Surah it is also mentioned that the followers of this message are those who avoid major sins and manage their affairs with mutual consultation.

## Commentary on Surah Al-Shura

1. Allah revealed His message to His Prophets. The purpose of revelation is to warn people about the Day of Judgment. Had Allah willed, He would have forced all people into one Ummah, but the wrong-doers will see the consequences of their deeds.

2. The judgment is in the hand of Allah. He gave the same religion to all His Prophets. Muslims must invite people to Allah.

3. Allah deals justly with all people. Allah accepts the repentant. Allah's mercy is manifest in the universe.

4. Believers should avoid sins, be patient, work with each other in consultation and practice forgiveness.

5. The Prophet guides to the right path, the path of Allah.

## 43. Surah Al-Zukhruf

This is a Makki Surah and it is fourth in number among the group of Surahs that begin with the word HaMim. It was revealed in the middle Makkan period. It has 89 verses in 7 sections.

The Surah tells us that the revelation is a mercy from Allah. Allah chooses whosoever He wills to give His revelation. Worldly possessions and riches do not necessarily mean that a person is best in the sight of Allah. The real value comes from following the truth and righteousness.

## Commentary on Surah Al-Zukhruf

1. This revelation is given to people in Arabic so that they may understand. The revelation is a mercy from Allah.

2. Shirk and blind following of ancestors are major problems of non-believers.

3. Allah chooses the Prophets and Messengers according to His wisdom. Worldly riches do not mean anything in the sight of Allah.

4. Those who forget Allah come under the influence of the Satan.

5. Pharaoh's response to Prophet Musa (Moses). Allah's punishment came against Pharaoh and his people.

6. Jesus' Message was also changed by some of his people.

7. The Believers will succeed in the Hereafter.

### 44. SURAH AL-DUKHAN

This is a Makki Surah and it is fifth in the number of Surahs that begin with HaMim. It has 59 verses in 3 sections.

The Surah warns about the punishment of Allah. When the punishment comes no one can avert it. The division between the righteous and wicked in the Hereafter will be the decision of Allah only.

### Commentary on Surah Al-Dukhan

1. The Qur'an is the book of warning.

2. The Day of Judgment is a certainty.

3. Allah will punish the wrongdoers and shall reward the righteous.

### 45. SURAH AL-JATHIYAH

This is a Makki Surah and it is the sixth among the Surahs that begin with HaMim. It has 37 verses in 4 sections. The Surah warns those who deny the Divine truth. It talks about human arrogance and sinfulness. The judgment of Allah will cover all the people. All the nations will kneel before him.

*Commentary on Surah Al-Jathiyah*
1. Allah's signs are all over in the universe and in our own soul. Those who deny the revelation of Allah will see His punishment.

2. Follow the clear path of truth.

3. Some people make their desires their god, and deny the Hereafter.

4. People will come before Allah on their knees. Their record of deeds will be presented to them.

## 46. SURAH AL-AHQAF

This is a Makki Surah—7th among the Surahs beginning with HaMim, and revealed in the middle Makkan period. It has 35 verses in 4 sections. The Surah warns those who deny the truth. When Allah's punishment comes, neither sea, nor dry land can protect. There is reference in the Surah to the people of 'Ad, and Allah's punishment for their sins.

*Commentary on Surah Al-Ahqaf*
1. Allah sent down the Qur'an and He has created the heaven and earth. The gods of Shirk have created nothing. Is there any proof for Shirk? The truth of this revelation is manifest.

2. The Qur'an verifies the previous revelations.

3. The fate of 'Ad.

4. Warnings to those who deny the truth. A group of Jinn accept the message. Be patient in giving the message of Allah.

## 47. SURAH MUHAMMAD

This is a Madani Surah; probably revealed in the first year of Hijrah, before the battle of Badr. It has 38 verses in 4 sections.
The Surah talks of the real struggle between truth and falsehood. The truth will be victorious, and falsehood and its votaries utterly defeated. Believers and those who deny the truth shall be separated.

*Commentary on Surah Muhammad*

1. Believers in Prophet Muhammad have their sins removed and their condition will improve. The opponents of the truth will perish.

2. Good news for the Believers. The Prophet is asked to pray for the Believers.

3. The weak and blind at heart are not able to see the truth.

4. The real success. Do not be intimidated, stand firm and struggle for the cause of Allah.

### 48. SURAH AL-FATH

This is a Madani Surah. According to 'Umar—may Allah be pleased with him—this Surah was revealed when Muslims were returning from the Hudaibiyah. The Treaty of Hudaibiyah took place in the 6th year of Hijrah. This Surah has 29 verses in 4 sections.

The Surah talks about the moral and physical victory of Islam over the forces of unbelief. The hypocrites and disbelievers will be disappointed with this victory.

*Commentary on Surah Al-Fath*

1. The victory that came through the Treaty of Peace at Hudaibiyah.

2. The hypocrites and their false excuses.

3. Allah is pleased with the Believers who are with the Prophet. Allah's promises for the Believers.

4. Ultimate triumph of Islam.

### 49. SURAH AL-HUJURAT

This is a Madani Surah. It was revealed around the 9th year of Hijrah when a large number of people embraced Islam. Many delegations were coming to visit Madinah to meet the Prophet—peace be upon him—to learn about Islam. The Surah has 18 verses in 2 sections.

The purpose of the Surah is to give Muslims teachings about social manners. How to respect their leader the Prophet—peace be upon him—and how to deal with each other. It has comprehensive guidelines to make a peaceful and harmonious society.

### Commentary on Surah Al-Hujurat

1. Respect of the Prophet. Proper manner of dealing with reports. Relations among the Believers.

2. Moral and ethical teachings to keep group harmony and solidarity. Relations with groups and tribes. Faith is a favour of Allah to the Believers.

### 50. SURAH QAF

This is a Makki Surah. This and the following six Surahs belong to the early Makkan period. This Surah has 45 verses in 3 sections. The Surah emphasizes the theme of resurrection and the ultimate success of those who have faith in Allah and His Prophets.

### Commentary on Surah Qaf

1. Nature points to the Resurrection.

2. Allah is closer to us than our life-vein. The death, the end of the world, and the Resurrection.

3. The Final judgment.

### 51. SURAH AL-DHARIYAT

This is a Makki Surah belonging to the early Makkan period. It has 60 verses in 3 sections. The Surah gives the good news of the emergence of a new community. It also warns the opponents of the truth that their time has come and the judgment of Allah is near.

*Commentary on Surah Al-Dhariyat*

1. Falsehood is about to end. The righteous shall be rewarded. The character of the righteous people.

2. Prophet Ibrahim (Abraham) and his angel visitors. The fate of the people of Prophet Lot. Prophet Musa (Moses) and the fate of Pharaoh. People of 'Ad and Thamud and the people of Prophet Noah—peace be upon them all.

3. Hasten to Allah. Do not associate any in the divinity of Allah. Remind! reminding helps the Believers. Allah's Judgment is near.

### 52. SURAH AL-TUR

This is a Makki Surah revealed in the early Makkan period. It has 49 verses in 2 sections. The Surah speaks about the mission of Prophet Muhammad—peace be upon him. He came to warn people about the consequences of their denial of faith and deeds of injustice and indecency. Those who doubt this message let them bring a similar message, and produce any proofs supporting their wrong beliefs.

*Commentary on Surah Al-Tur*

1. Warnings about Allah's coming punishment for the disbelievers. Reward for the Believers.

2. Questions to the disbelievers about their false beliefs. What are the evidences and proofs of these false beliefs?

### 53. SURAH AL-NAJM

This is a Makki Surah revealed in the early Makkan period. It has 62 verses in 3 sections. The Surah talks about the eminence of the Prophet—peace be upon him—with his Mi'raj and closeness to Allah. It warns the disbelievers about the errors of their attitude towards the Qur'an and the Prophet of Allah. Some of their wrong beliefs in; the angels as daughters of Allah, intercession of the angels… are also mentioned.

## Commentary on Surah Al-Najm

1. The Mi'raj experience of the Prophet Muhammad—peace be upon him. Gods or goddesses of the non-believers are mere conjecture and names without any basis in fact or reality.

2. The angels are servants of Allah. No intercession can work against Allah. Allah is most forgiving, but He requires righteousness.

3. Those who deny the truth confront Allah's power and majesty.

### 54. SURAH AL-QAMAR

This is a Makki Surah revealed in the early Makkan period. It has 55 verses in 3 sections. The Surah talks about the approaching Day of Judgment. It describes some scenes of that Day. It also tells us that Allah's judgment may come here and now. There are references to the flood that came at the time of Prophet Noah, the punishment of the people of 'Ad, Thamud, People of Prophet Lot, the Pharaoh and his people. It ends with the good news for the Believers who will be near their Lord in the gardens of bliss.

## Commentary on Surah Al-Qamar

1. The Day of Judgment is near. References to Prophet Noah, and to the tribe of 'Ad,

2. References to the Thamud tribe, Prophet Lot and his people.

3. Pharaoh and his arrogance. The opponents in Makkah are told whether they think they are better or more powerful than those nations. The wrongdoers did suffer the consequences of their evil deeds.

### 55. SURAH AL-RAHMAN

Scholarly opinion differs on whether this is a Makki or Madani Surah; to some this is a Makki Surah revealed during the early Makkan period. The Surah has 78 verses in 3 sections. The Surah clearly indicates that Prophet Muhammad is Allah's Prophet and Messenger for humans as well as Jinns. Allah's many blessings and favours are mentioned in this Surah. Humans and Jinn are invited to remember these favours and not deny Allah's blessings.

## Commentary on Surah Al-Rahman

1. The various bounties of Allah.

2. Everything is finite, but Allah is infinite. Everyone depends on Allah. The warnings to the guilty.

3. The rewards for the righteous.

## 56. Surah Al-Waqi'ah

This is a Makki Surah from the early Makkan period of 96 verses in 3 sections. It is the seventh of the group of Surahs that began with Qaf (no. 50). It completes the subject of death, resurrection and divine judgment. The Surah talks about the resurrection that will definitely take place—a fact undeniable. Humans will fall into three distinct groups. The faithful are two types: those pioneering and foremost in their faith, and those struggling in the path of Allah. They are a large number from amongst the earlier community, and a small number from the later generations. The remaining people are believers and those who opposed the faith. Allah's rewards are for the faithful and his anger and chastisement await the opponents of faith. The Surah then invites human beings to think about themselves and the things they use daily, and consider who created all these things. It talks about the Qur'an —its profound and consistent message, and finally reminds of death and the coming end of every living thing.

## Commentary on Surah Al-Waqi'ah

1. The reality will come to pass. Humanity will be in three camps: people of the right hand, people of the left hand and the foremost in faith. The reward of the believers.

2. The guilty and their punishment. Arguments about the Tawhid and Akhirah (hereafter).

3. The Qur'an and its consistent message. Reminder about death, divine judgment and the reward and punishment.

### 57. SURAH AL-HADID

This is a Madani Surah revealed between the 4th and 5th year of Hijrah—time between the Battle of Badr and the Treaty of Hudaibiyah. The Surah has 29 verses in 4 sections.

The Surah was revealed during the period when the non-believers attacked the tiny Islamic State from all sides. It encourages Muslims to make sacrifices for their faith and be aware of the non-believers as well as the hypocrites in their own ranks.

### *Commentary on Surah Al-Hadid*

1. All knowledge and authority belongs to Allah; have faith in Allah's power, make sacrifice and give charity for the cause of truth.

2. Light and Life are for the Believers. The disbelievers walk in darkness. Warning to those who refuse to acknowledge Allah. Sincere in faith are those willing to sacrifice and help the poor and needy.

3. The life of this world is temporary. Compete with each other in doing good things to receive the eternal reward from Allah. Prophets were sent to establish justice with authority.

4. References to Prophets Noah, Ibrahim (Abraham), and Jesus— peace be upon them all. All Prophets preached the same message, but some of their followers went to extremes. The Christians thus invented monasticism for themselves. It was not commanded by Allah. The Believers are asked to have faith and walk in the light of Allah. The final success belongs to the Believers.

**58. SURAH AL-MUJADALAH**
This is a Madani Surah. It was revealed around the 5th year of Hijrah after the Battle of the Ditch. This Surah most probably came after Surah al-Ahzab (33). It has 22 verses in 3 sections.

The Surah talks about a bad social custom by which husbands in pre-Islamic times used to oppress their wives. Someone would call his wife "mother" and thus would separate from her, but would not give her divorce. Allah condemned this custom. The Surah also speaks about the hypocrites and other non-Muslim groups in Madinah who were involved in spreading rumours against the Prophet—peace be upon him. They are given warnings here and Muslims are urged to be alert and careful.

*Commentary on Surah Al-Mujadalah*
1. The custom of Zihar (an old Pagan custom for divorce) is condemned. The rights of women should be protected.

2. Allah is aware of the secret councils of the hypocrites. Believers should not be involved in such activities. The rules of gatherings in Islam.

3. Be aware of the internal enemies also. Do not take as patrons those who are the enemies of Allah and His Messenger.

**59. SURAH AL-HASHR**
This is a Madani Surah revealed after the banishment of the Jewish tribe of Bani Nadhir from Madinah. This took place after the Battle of Uhud in the 4th year of Hijrah. This Surah has 24 verses in 3 sections.

The Surah talks about the banishment of Bani Nadhir and secret relations between them and the hypocrites of Madinah. It exhorts the Believers to be firm in their faith in Allah and gives some of the Beautiful Names of Allah.

*Commentary on Surah Al-Hashr*

1. The Banishment of the Jewish tribe of Bani Nadhir. The distribution of the spoils.

2. The false promises of the hypocrites.

3. The exhortation of the Believers to faith. The Beautiful Names of Allah.

### 60. SURAH AL-MUMTAHINAH

This is a Madani Surah. It was revealed after the Treaty of Hudaibiyah and before the conquest of Makkah in the 6th or 7th year of Hijrah. It has 13 verses in 2 sections.

The Surah deals with the relations of Muslims with non-Muslims. It tells Muslims on the one hand not to take the enemies of Allah as their allies and patrons, but on the other hand it tells them not to consider every non-Muslim as their enemy.

*Commentary on Surah Al-Mumtahinah*

1. Do not take Allah's and your own enemies as patrons and allies.

2. It is allowed to have friendly relations with those non-Muslims who do not fight you for your religion and do not expel you from your lands. Rules on women who migrated to Madinah, and their husbands had not accepted Islam.

### 61. SURAH AL-SAFF

This is a Madani Surah revealed probably in the first or second year of Hijrah. It has 14 verses in 2 sections.

The Surah exhorts Muslims to defend the truth. It tells them that this may involve fighting the enemies who may come to attack Muslims. The Surah speaks about Prophet Musa (Moses) and his difficulties with his own people. He told them to follow Allah's rules and they did not listen to him. Then Allah sent Jesus among them and he also reminded them about Allah and gave them the good news of the coming of Prophet Muhammad—peace be upon all the prophets and Messengers of Allah. But they continue in their stubborn denial. The Surah ends with the good news that the true religion will prevail in the end and Allah will give it victory.

## Commentary on Surah Al-Saff

1. Struggle for the Truth. The light of Islam will shine more.

2. The way of success for the believers is to struggle for the truth.

### 62. SURAH AL-JUMU'AH

This is a Madani Surah. It seems that the first part of this Surah was revealed in the 7th year of Hijrah after the Battle of Khaybar and the second part was revealed soon after the Hijrah in the 1st year of Hijrah. The Surah has 11 verses in 2 sections.

The Surah talks about the negligence of Bani Israel in obeying the commands of Allah and becoming too involved in worldly matters. They only carried the Books of Allah, but failed to follow these books. Muslims are urged to observe the Friday prayer and not transact business so much as to neglect the remembrance of Allah.

## Commentary on Surah Al-Jumu'ah

1. Allah's favour upon Muslims that Allah sent His Prophet among them to teach them and to purify them. Bani Israel neglected the commands of Allah.

2. Muslims are exhorted to observe the Friday prayers and always remember Allah.

### 63. SURAH AL-MUNAFIQUN

This is a Madani Surah revealed around the 6th year of Hijrah. It has 11 verses in 2 sections. The Surah deals with the phenomenon of hypocrisy. It criticizes hypocrisy and condemns the hypocrites. It also exhorts the Believers to be sincere in their faith and give charity.

*Commentary on Surah Al-Munafiqun*

1. Criticism of hypocrisy.

2. Exhortation to the Believers.

### 64. SURAH AL-TAGHABUN

This is a Madani Surah revealed during the early Madinah period. It has 18 verses in 2 sections. The Surah invites to faith, obedience of Allah and good morals. It warns about the evil consequences of misdeeds and about the coming of the Day of Judgment when the real success or loss will be manifest.

*Commentary on Surah Al-Taghabun*

1. Allah created human beings; some among them are believers and some non-believers. He knows everything. He sent His Prophets to warn and remind. Remember the Day of Judgment.

2. Believe in Allah, purify your motives and be generous in giving for the cause of Allah.

### 65. SURAH AL-TALAQ

This is a Madani Surah revealed in the 6th year of Hijrah. It has 12 verses in 2 sections. This and Surah al-Tahrim following it, address family rules. Spouses should follow Allah's rules whether they are in disagreement, or love each other. In this Surah, the proper rules of divorce are given. Do not just say the words of divorce and separate yourself from your wives, but give them their rights. It also reminds the Believers to obey Allah and His Messenger. Those who disobey Allah are warned of the consequences of their disobedience.

*Commentary on Surah Al-Talaq*

1. The Rules of Divorce.

2. Warning to those who disobey the commands of Allah.

## 66. SURAH AL-TAHRIM

This is a Madani Surah revealed around the 7th year of Hijrah. It has 12 verses in 2 sections. The Surah tells spouses not to ignore Allah's rules in their love for each other. It refers to an incident that took place between the Prophet and his wives. This incident is used to instruct the Believers to understand the nature of Halal (permitted) and Haram (prohibited) and to understand that the success and salvation in the Hereafter will not be based on family or tribal relations, but purely on faith in Allah.

### Commentary on Surah Al-Tahrim

1. The rules of Allah are supreme. Save yourselves and your families from the hellfire.

2. Allah requires true repentance. Salvation is not based on family or tribal relations, but on Iman and Taqwa.

## 67. SURAH AL-MULK

This and the following ten are Makki Surahs, which were revealed in the early Makkan period. The emphasis in all these Surahs is on faith and Allah's message that has come through His last Prophet Muhammad. Although these Surahs were revealed at the very beginning of the Prophet's work in Makkah, they contain prophecies, sometimes plainly and sometimes in metaphorical language, about the success of the truth.

Surah Mulk has 30 verses in 2 sections. It talks about the greatness of Allah and beautiful universe that He has created. It reminds people that if they consider the laws of the universe and travel in the land with open eyes, they will indeed see that this whole kingdom belongs to Allah and He controls everything.

## 68. SURAH AL-QALAM

This Surah has 52 verses in 2 sections. The Surah tells us that the message of the Prophet is not the talk of a madman. The writings of all scriptures bear testimony to the truth of this message. It urges people to be charitable and help the poor and needy. The story of the people of a garden is mentioned; they wished to deny charity to the poor and suffered the consequences in losing everything. The Surah ends with the story of Prophet Jonah—peace be upon him. It urges the Prophet and hence his followers to continue this mission and not give up in frustration. The mission of Islam is for the whole world.

## 69. SURAH AL-HAQQAH

This Surah has 52 verses in 2 sections. The Surah tells of the fate of Thamud, 'Ad, Pharaoh, other overthrown towns, and the flood in the time of Prophet Noah. It talks about the reward of the faithful and the punishment of disbelievers. At the end, it reminds the people that this message is not poetry of a poet, or something made up by the Prophet himself, rather the revelation of the Lord of the worlds.

## 70. SURAH AL-MA'ARIJ

The Surah has 44 verses in 2 sections. It talks about the ways of the ascent of the Believers. The rise of truth will be gradual, but it is sure. The Surah talks about the problems of human beings in general, but those who believe their character is different. It warns about the coming doom of the disbelievers.

## 71. SURAH NUH

This Surah has 28 verses in 2 sections. This Surah talks about the preaching of Prophet Noah and then his prayer for the destruction of the disbelievers. Thus Allah's wrath came upon them and they were all destroyed in a flood.

## 72. Surah Al-Jinn

This Surah has 28 verses in 2 sections. The Surah gives assurance
that the message of Allah will be accepted. It talks about some Jinn
who accepted the message and so predicts that if the present people
deny the message, then others, unseen, will accept it.

## 73. Surah Al-Muzammil

This Surah has 20 verses in 2 sections. The Surah emphasized prayers
and the reading of the Qur'an in prayers. It tells the Prophet and
all those who stand to preach the message of Allah to take their
strength from the word of Allah. Read the Qur'an and spend your
wealth in the path of Allah.

## 74. Surah Al-Mudathir

This Surah has 56 verses in 2 sections. The subject of this Surah is
Da'wah to Islam. The Prophet and his followers are told to stand up
to remove the evils and vices from the society. It also gives warnings
of the coming doom for those who deny the truth.

## 75. Surah Al-Qiyamah

This Surah has 40 verses in 2 sections. It talks about the spiritual
resurrection of the soul when it becomes aware of its Lord and the
physical resurrection that takes place at the end of the world.

## 76. Surah Al-Dahr

This Surah also called al-Insan has 31 verses in 2 sections. It presents
ways of attaining growth and spiritual development. The rewards of
the Believers and their character is also mentioned.

## 77. Surah Al-Mursalat

This Surah has 50 verses in 2 sections. While the previous Surah
told how the Believers gain moral and spiritual perfection, this Surah
mentions the downfall and destruction of the rejecters of the truth.

**78. Surah Al-Naba'**
This and the remaining Surahs, except Surah 110, are Makki Surahs.
They were revealed in the early Makkan period. This Surah has 40
verses in 2 sections. The Surah gives important news or a message. It
tells us that the Day of Decision is coming. This beautiful and orderly
universe points to the Day of Decision. Allah will bring all people to
judgment. The wicked will be thrown in hell, and the righteous will
receive their reward from Allah.

**79. Surah Al-Nazi'at**
This Surah has 46 verses in 2 sections. It speaks about Allah's angels
who take the souls at the time of death. Allah has power to take
away the souls, as He has created the whole universe, He also has
the power to resurrect people after their death. The story of Prophet
Musa (Moses) and Pharaoh is mentioned to warn the people of the
consequences of arrogant pride, which leads to denial of the truth.

**80. Surah 'Abasa**
This Surah has 42 verses in 1 section. The Surah begins with the
incident of a blind man (Abdullah ibn Umm Maktum) who came
to the Prophet to seek knowledge, while the chiefs of Makkah were
denying the message. It talks about the greatness of Allah's message.
Those who accept this message, will benefit from it, and those who
deny this message bring harm to their own selves.

**81. Surah Al-Takwir**
This Surah has 29 verses in 1 section. The Surah talks about the end
of the world. Very powerfully, it describes scenes of the Last Day.
All the natural, as well as human power and authority will come to
an end. This is a serious message, not the words of a madman. The
purpose is to remind people to become morally upright.

### 82. SURAH AL-INFITAR

This Surah has 19 verses in 1 section. The Surah reminds human beings that Allah has given them a wonderful proportionate shape, but they and the whole universe are totally dependent upon Allah. The creation has a purpose and the Day of Judgment will come.

### 83. SURAH AL-MUTAFFIFIN

This Surah has 36 verses in 1 section. The Surah warns those who commit fraud in business. It reminds of honest dealings. The righteous will prosper. Allah has the record of every person.

### 84. SURAH AL-INSHIQAQ

This Surah has 25 verses in 1 section. This Surah tells us that this world has no permanence. It also speaks about the record of deeds and the rewards of the righteous and the punishment of the wicked. It reminds people to pay attention to the Qur'an.

### 85. SURAH AL-BURUJ

This Surah has 22 verses in 1 section. The Surah speaks about the persecution of the Believers. Allah watches over His own people and He will bring His enemies to judgment. The Surah warns the opponents of this message. Their end might be like many nations in the past, who denied Allah's message and persecuted the Believers.

### 86. AL-TARIQ

This Surah has 17 verses in 1 section. Everything in this universe is working under the protection and supervision of the great Keeper. The creation of human beings as well as the creation of this universe is not a joke. The creation is the serious work of Allah and so is His word, the Qur'an.

**87. SURAH AL-A'LA**

This Surah has 19 verses in 1 section. The Surah speaks about the praise of Allah the Most High. He created everything. He created the human being and gave him capacity to make progress. Man can make progress if he obeys Allah's rules. The Qur'an is the message from Allah and He will guard it. The Prophet should continue giving the message to others. Those who accept it will benefit from it, but those who reject it will be the losers. It talks about the 'Akhirah and that this message is the same that was given to Prophets Ibrahim (Abraham) and Musa (Moses)—peace be upon them.

**88. SURAH AL-GHASHIYAH**

This Surah has 26 verses in 1 section. The Surah talks about the coming calamity that will overwhelm everything. Humanity will be divided into two groups: the frightened, tired and exhausted group, and the joyful and happy group. Then attention is drawn to this wonderful creation of Allah. The Prophet is told to remind people. His mission is to remind only, not to impose the message. Allah will make the conclusive judgment.

**89. SURAH AL-FAJR**

This Surah has 30 verses in 1 section. The Surah talks about the judgment of Allah: the reward and punishment that will take place in the hereafter.

**90. SURAH AL-BALAD**

This Surah has 20 verses in 1 section. It begins with a reference to the city of Makkah, where the Prophet was going through an experience of pain and suffering due to the denial of his people. It talks about the different stages of human life. This world is not the place of real comfort. This life is the test for human beings to do good deeds and then the final judgment will be in the Hereafter.

### 91. SURAH AL-SHAMS

This Surah has 15 verses in 1 section. The Surah tells us that as there is a contrast between sun and moon, night and day, heaven and earth, so there is also a big difference between good and evil.

### 92. SURAH AL-LAYL

This Surah has 21 verses in 1 section. Basically, it has the same theme as the previous Surah, but it tells us about the two ways of life—the good and the evil—and the consequences of both.

### 93. SURAH AL-DHUHA

This Surah has 11 verses in 1 section. This Surah gives a message of hope and consolation. It reminds about Allah's blessings and the way the Believers should take these blessings.

### 94. SURAH AL-INSHIRAH

This Surah has 8 verses in 1 section. The Surah tells us that the Believers should not give up under difficulties and stress. There will be ease after difficulty.

### 95. SURAH AL-TIN

This Surah has 8 verses in 1 section. Four historic events are mentioned and the conclusion drawn that Allah's judgment will come.

### 96. SURAH AL-'ALAQ

This Surah has 19 verses in 1 section. The first five verses are among the first revealed to the Prophet—peace be upon him—in the cave of Hira. The rest of the Surah was revealed when the message was publicised to the people of Makkah and they began threatening the Prophet. The Surah speaks about the humble beginning of humans, yet the high position they atain by following the message of Allah.

**97. SURAH AL-QADR**
This Surah has 5 verses in 1 section. The Surah talks about the majesty and glory of the Qur'an and the time of its revelation.

**98. SURAH AL-BAYYINAH**
This Surah has 8 verses in 1 section. The Surah tells us that Prophet Muhammad came with a clear message and a Divine Book. This Book (the Qur'an) contains the basic message of all the Prophets of Allah. It also draws attention to the different ends of those who follow the right path and those who turn away from the truth.

**99. SURAH AL-ZILZAL**
This Surah has 8 verses in 1 section. This Surah talks about life after death and that all deeds will be exposed on the Day of Judgment.

**100. SURAH AL-'ADIYAT**
This Surah has 11 verses in 1 section. The Surah tells us of the ungratefulness of man and where it leads him. It describes the wild and unruly lifestyle of the Arabs before Islam. It reminds that Allah knows all the hidden secrets of human souls and He will expose them on the Day of Judgment.

**101. SURAH AL-QARI'AH**
This Surah has 11 verses in 1 section. The Surah gives the warning about the Day of Judgment. It will be the day of great clamour. People will be scattered and the mountains will crumble. Only those whose balance of good deeds will be heavy will prosper.

**102. SURAH AL-TAKATHUR**
This Surah has 8 verses in 1 section. The Surah talks about the evil consequences of materialism and this worldliness.

### 103. SURAH AL-'ASR

This Surah has 3 Verses in 1 section. The Surah tells us that generally humans are losers; then describes the way to success and salvation.

### 104. SURAH AL-HUMAZAH

This Surah has 9 verses in 1 section. The Surah talks about some of the moral problems that affect the wealthy and then it gives them warnings of the consequences of these evils.

### 105. SURAH AL-FIL

This Surah has 5 verses in 1 section. The Surah reminds of the event when the Ka'bah was attacked by an army from the Southern part of Arabia, but Allah destroyed that army. It is the same God who protected the Ka'bah, His message is now conveyed by Prophet Muhammad -peace be upon him.

### 106. SURAH QURAISH

This Surah has 4 verses in 1 section. It reminded the people of Makkah that it was Allah who gave them honour and prestige among other tribes due to His House, the Ka'bah, so why not worship Him and obey His command. Similarly, it is a reminder to others to worship Allah who provides everything.

### 107. SURAH AL-MA'UN

This Surah has 7 verses in 1 section. Religion means social service; helping the poor and needy. The Surah tells us that the true belief in Allah and the last day create a kind and compassionate character.

### 108. SURAH AL-KAWTHAR

This Surah has 3 verses in 1 section. The Surah gives good news and comfort that Allah's message will prevail and the enemies of the truth will be the losers.

## 109. SURAH AL-KAFIRUN

This Surah has 6 verses in 1 section. The Surah tells us that there cannot be any compromise in the matters of faith and worship. People are free to follow whatever religion they want, but the truth and falsehood cannot be mixed together.

## 110. SURAH AL-NASR

This Surah has 3 verses in 1 section. This is a Madani Surah and according to most of the authorities is the last Surah revealed to the Prophet -peace be upon him. The Surah reminds about the attitude of the Believer in the situation of success. One should be thankful to Allah and seek His forgiveness for any shortcomings or mistakes.

## 111. SURAH AL-LAHAB

This Surah has 5 verses in 1 section. This Surah was revealed to condemn the behaviour of one of the relatives of the Prophet who stood against his message. The Surah gives a warning that those who oppose the message of Allah, they will be severely punished, regardless whether they are of the family of the Prophet or not.

## 112. SURAH AL-IKHLAS

This Surah has 4 verses in 1 section. This is a great Surah of Tawhid. It speaks about the oneness of Allah.

## 113. SURAH AL-FALAQ

This Surah has 5 verses in 1 section. The Surah reminds us that evil is lurking everywhere and anything can become harmful. One should always be conscious, do right things and seek Allah's protection.

## 114. SURAH AL-NAS

This Surah has 6 verses in 1 section. The Surah tells us that Satan is always against the human beings and he puts wrong suggestions in their minds. We should seek Allah's protection from Satan and his whisperings. This is a very appropriate ending for the Book of Allah. The Book of Allah is to provide protection from all evil and give success under the guidance of Allah.